ISBN-10: 1975994051
ISBN-13: 978-1975994051

The JRS Realty Group™ Real Estate Advisors

JRSRealtyGroup.com
ListWithJohnSalkowski.com
PriceInYourNeighborhood.com
PhiladelphiaAreaHomeSearch.com

SOLD!

LISTING TO CLOSING

The Ultimate Home Sellers Guide

JOHN SALKOWSKI

To my beautiful daughter, Alexa Marie.
The love of my life, my best friend - my Why Power.

It's because of you that I work tirelessly to achieve more and to be more. I continually strive to set good examples both, personally and professionally so you too can attain great things in your life.

I love you.

This book is written with so much gratitude in my heart for every client who has entrusted me with their largest financial and emotional investment - their home.

I am forever grateful to each of you for your trust.

ALSO BY JOHN SALKOWSKI

LEADERSHIP IN THE LINE OF DUTY™
50 Leadership Lessons for Making Split-Second Decisions
from a Cop Who Has Been in Life and Death Situations

SUCCESS THOUGHTS AND QUOTES FOR LEADERS

NOTHING BUT NET
Step Up to a Whole New Level of Success

WHAT CLIENTS ARE SAYING ABOUT
JOHN SALKOWSKI

After a Year on the Market - John SOLD Our Home in Three Days!

"After 365 days on the market with another Realtor and no offers, we were frustrated to say the least. We never thought our home would sell. We received several mailers from John that were very impressive. So, we decided to call John and invite him over. We interviewed a total of five agents and we must say John Salkowski stood out by far. His professionalism, knowledge and businessman savvy made him our top choice. He had wonderful pre-sale suggestions and even helped stage the house for the new listing. Our home went on the market on a Tuesday and by Friday, just three days later our home was sold at 99 percent of list price! John priced our home exactly where it was previously for one year. John was confident that he could sell our home at a very good price. His skill at negotiating with the buyer resulted in a very good deal for us. I highly recommend John if you want a Realtor you can depend on, will answer your questions, be available when you need him and will get the best deal and results possible when negotiating the sale. And, he also managed to get us a great deal on our newly-purchased townhouse. Amazing businessman and Realtor!"

– Joanne & Kevin Reilly

BOOM! SOLD in 18 days!

"Our home was on the market for 131 days with another Realtor with five showings and no offers before expiring. As soon as our home was removed from the market we received an intriguing mailer from John Salkowski. He sent us his impressive flyer and a MLS sheet of our property with so many mistakes and horrible pictures. We decided to call John over for an interview. In addition, we interviewed a total of four agents. We knew immediately upon meeting John that he was the man for the job. We could tell by his demeanor, professionalism and confidence level that our house would sell, that we could entrust him to get our home sold. We were under contract in 18 days with John. All of the paperwork was handled by him with ease and convenience and we would recommend John to anyone and everyone who wants to sell their home quickly and at a great price."

– Wendell and Adeline Parson

John Salkowski

On Your Side

"John is the real estate professional you want on your side. After having our custom home listed for over a year and a half, we hired John after reading about him on-line. He was extremely professional, energetic and optimistic about being able to sell our home. We met with many challenges, but John was always available and encouraging. If you want an agent who knows the business and is always available, John is your man. Thank you so much, John."

– Renee Byrne

"Constant Foot Traffic

"I had previously tried to sell the house through another Realtor who didn't seem to understand the area as well as the uniqueness of the house. That was not the case with John. He understood how to price and market the house accordingly. I had constant foot traffic while the house was on the market. I would recommend him to anyone trying to sell a home in Delaware County! Thanks John!"

- **Liz Crafton**

Marketing Strategist and Partner

"Making the decision to list our home was a tough one that took well over a year. John was with us every step of the way. He never failed to return our calls, answer questions, even made visits to our house. Needless to say, once we decided to list our home, we hired John. Just 24-hours later our house was under agreement! John is more than a real estate agent ... he's a marketing strategist and partner who is willing to put in the work to get his clients the best price."

- Charlie McDermott

Market Expertise and Tenacity

"John helped sell one of my properties in three weeks after I had it listed with another broker for 6 months. His market expertise and tenacity in representing me, as a client, was unmatched. I listed another property with John a short time later and it sold very quickly as well. I was unable to make the closing and John orchestrated all necessary efforts for me to still sell the property. I would highly recommend John to anyone in need of real estate services."

- Mark Cooke

Incredibly Patient

"I met John when my wife and I were looking for our first home. We had been searching on our own for a while and were in a pinch to find something relatively quick. Thankfully Google pointed us to John. His energy and enthusiasm are incredible. Not only did he find us the perfect home at a great price, I now count him as a friend. If you are looking for an honest, hard-working agent to sell your home of if you are looking to find your next dream home – look no further. John is the person you want on your side of the negotiating table. Integrity, honesty, loyalty – and so much more - that's John Salkowski."

- Andy Keenan

A Man of Excellence

"John took over my listing after a big name realtor company who closed their doors in my area just weeks into the process. I called John the same day my previous realtor went AWOL. John was at my home early the next day. We sat down and John assured me he could take care of everything from listing to closing and everything in between. From the moment I met John I knew he was a man of excellence and honor. Traits not usually found in a Realtor. His professionalism and knowledge of real estate far exceed any of his competitors. I left my home in John's hands and moved out of state. John kept me updated weekly on showings, local price averages in my area and suggestions on how to improve our listing. Before I knew it John had my home sold at a great price. I returned for the closing just so I could thank John in person. John is a person to be trusted with your home. He treats your home as if he was selling his own."

- Chuck & Michele Kane

Just Awesome

"John Salkowski was just awesome. He guided us every step of the way in selling our home. Starting from the moment he came to our home to help us sell our house, we knew he was the person to help us through the process. No matter where he was if we called with a question, he got back to us right away. He was always cheerful, and has a very positive personality and very professional. He is #1 with us, and I would recommend him to anyone who is looking to sell or buy. Thank you John, you're the best!"

- John & Sue Penna

TABLE OF CONTENTS

INTRODUCTION

The Reason I Wrote this Book

PART ONE: SHOULD YOU OR SHOULDN'T YOU?

- Should I Sell?
- Your Most Important Questions
- First Things First – Sell or Buy?
- Use Same Broker to Sell and Buy?
- What Makes A Home Sell?
- When Is The Best Time To Sell?
- Is There A Better Time To Sell?
- Price Trends, Interest Rates and the Economy
- What If I Don't Have Money To Invest Into A Renovation?
- Does Name & Size of Real Estate Company Matter?

PART TWO: MONEY TALKS – IT REALLY DOES

- How Important Is Pricing Your Home?
- "I Can Always Lower The Price …"
- Pricing It Right The First Time
- Things To Consider

PART THREE: GETTIN' READY

- Our Selling Secrets
- What Happens At The Curb Matters
- Do's and Don'ts of Over-Improving Your Home
- Improvements to Avoid If You Plan To Sell Your Home
- Improvements to Make if You Plan to Stay in Your Home
- Improvements to Make if You Plan to Sell
- Preparing Your Home For Photography
- Must-Do's Before Showing Your Home
- Why a Pre-Sale Home Inspection is an Investment – Not an Expense

PART FOUR: MARKETING - TIME TO GO TO WORK

- Important Reasons to Hire a Real Estate Professional
- Not All Real Estate Agents Are The Same
- What Happens on Social Media Matters
- Individual Agent vs. Team Structure
- Why You Should Think Again About Selling on Your Own
- Why We Discourage Your "Traditional" Open House
- Not Your Typical Realtor
- John Salkowski By The Numbers
- No Seller Left Behind - How to Take the Stress Out of Distressed Sales
- What Senior Citizens Should Know About Selling Their Home

PART FIVE: PUTTING IT ON PAPER

- All About Offers, Counter Offers, and Contingencies
- What You Need to Know about Closing
- Estimate of Seller's Closing Costs
- Estimate of Buyer's Closing Costs

PART SIX: MOVING ON UP!

- Gearing Up for Moving Day - Moving Checklist
- Tips for Working with Professional Movers
- Packing Tips

REAL ESTATE DICTIONARY

ANNUAL HOME MAINTENANCE

SOME FINAL WORDS

TRUSTED ADVISORS

ABOUT JOHN SALKOWSKI

INTRODUCTION

THE REASON I WROTE THIS BOOK

Selling a home is and will be one of the largest financial and emotional transactions one can go through in their lifetime. It is and can be a very confusing, complicated process with an enormous amount of liability. Especially if you don't have a tried and true professional by your side – one that has helped hundreds upon hundreds, if not thousands of other sellers just like yourself.

I liken this process to a very serious surgical procedure – it may be needed, but it could also bring a high risk with it. You would certainly want a second, third and perhaps even a fourth opinion to make sure that you are making the right decision in selecting a surgeon. It needs to be someone who is not only in the top 1 percent in his or her field, but one who has also has performed hundreds, if not thousands of these same procedures with success. Selling your home must be taken just as serious.

Here's why.

If you select the wrong agent, it will undoubtedly cost you thousands of dollars and more importantly, valuable time. We all know that time is the most precious of commodities that we have and once that time passes, we cannot get it back. It is my passion and purpose to educate you with every ounce of my being during this process.

We'll cover the vital tools you'll need in your home-selling arsenal, such as:

- How much to ask for your home
- How to understand which home improvement projects are worth making or not making
- How to get your home ready for showings in person as well as online
- How to successfully and strategically structure your personalized marketing plan on your home
- Our negotiation tactics that puts us and keeps us in the driver's seat

My goal for you is to use this book as a tool, along with sound advice from a real estate broker - not just a real estate agent (and believe me, there is a difference) - utilizing their experience, integrity, number of transactions and positive reviews from happy clients who can help you sell your home and guide you through the transition process.

You have my promise to hold your hand through each step of this process, from our initial meeting to sitting with you at the closing table. I will help you get your home ready to sell and help you achieve your goal of selling it fast and for top dollar.

You have my personal guarantee.

PART ONE

SHOULD YOU OR SHOULDN'T YOU?

DECISIONS ... DECISIONS

"There are many reasons why someone decides to sell their home, however; one must remember this is a process, not an event."

– John Salkowski

Should I Sell?

There are many circumstances in life that may dictate why you may decide to sell your home. Some might be under your direct control, and some may not. Some involve your stage of life with your job and family. Others might be dictated by financial factors, like losing a job, going through a divorce, no longer being able to afford the mortgage and are behind on payments or … it's just time to move on.

Relocating

This might happen when you or your spouse secures a new job in a different state. You may be offered a job that will enhance your career and ultimately enable you to provide better for your family. Or, perhaps you've been out of work for months or years, and you land a job out of town or state.

Up-Sizing or Down-Sizing

If your family is growing, you may need that extra bedroom or more square footage, extra garage space, a home office, attic, a finished basement with a walkout or a larger backyard. Maybe you're in a situation in which an aging parent(s) will be moving in with you so you can care for them. Once you retire and the kids are grown and gone, it may be time to downsize and start the next chapter. You may also want to move to a warmer climate or closer to your kids. There may be other factors that play a part however these may just be a few.

Financial Stress

This can occur if you, or your spouse, have lost a job. Maybe you have a family member who is very ill, and you've accumulated hefty medical expenses. Perhaps you're going through a divorce or the death of a spouse. These types of events often alter your financial situation and may require you to move to a smaller home or perhaps rent.

Your Most Important Questions

As you contemplate selling your home, you'll likely have many questions. If you've never sold a house before, it can be overwhelming and confusing. It's my passion to help you understand and guide you through this process.

First Things First – Sell or Buy?

A big dilemma amongst sellers is whether to sell or buy first. It really depends on your financial situation. This is a conversation to have during your initial consultation.

I have helped sellers sell first and buy first. Either way, it takes an experienced professional to coordinate both closings simultaneously. If you sell first, you will know exactly how much money you'll have to work with on your purchase. However, if you sell first and don't have a home to go to, where will you live until you purchase?

The most concerning component for sellers is the potential of carrying two mortgages. As I mentioned above, it truly depends on your financial situation. You also don't have to worry that you may have to temporarily carry two mortgage payments as well as everything else that comes along with having a mortgage, such as maintenance costs, as well as insurance and property tax payments. But selling first also means you may feel rushed into buying. If you don't find a house you like, you may have to rent until you do. That means you will have to move more than once and you may have to put belongings in storage.

Here is what I suggest to my clients.

Before preparing your home for sale, I get my clients pre-approved through a trusted mortgage lender. This way, they will know exactly what they can afford on their next home, as well as finding out if they can buy first or if they need to sell first. Once this process is complete, we then prepare their home for sale. Next, I have them looking at homes online through our proprietary buyer portal to see what they like and where they want to live. Once they have this narrowed down, we then place their home on the market. While the home is on the market, I have them out looking at homes.

An experienced professional will help you make the transition from selling to buying as smooth as possible, usually having simultaneous closings, with the home they're selling first and then later in the day, the home their buying.

Allow me to stress. Not every agent can do this with precision. This is why you must choose an experienced professional.

See what some of our clients have to say - www.JRSRavingReviews.com.

Should I use the same broker to sell and buy?

It can be a daunting process if you decide to use two different brokers to sell and buy. Obviously, if you are relocating this is a must, however; communication between both brokers is paramount.

If you are staying local, then we highly suggest you work with the broker who is selling your home. It just makes the process run smoothly. The broker knows your situation, what you can afford in your next home and how much equity you are working with. Trust is obviously important, however if you have entrusted the broker to sell your home, I am certain you will trust them to assist you in your purchase. I'll repeat this numerous times throughout the book - You must work with an experienced professional.

What makes a home sell?

The most important factors are price, condition, staging, location, terms, marketing, communication, negotiating and exposure.

When is the best time to sell?

The best time to sell is as soon as you decide to. If you want to receive top dollar for your home, it's important to give yourself as much time as possible to get the home ready.

Unless you absolutely want or need to sell your home in as-is condition, the more time to prepare your home means more potential buyers have a chance to see your home, ultimately resulting in more offers and more options for you.

Is there a better time to sell?

Peak selling seasons vary from year to year in our area. Weather often plays a role in the market. In many parts of the country, early spring and early fall are the most popular seasons. However, there tends to be more competition during these times as well. People generally like to go house hunting when the weather is pleasant. They also prefer to be moved in by the holidays and by the end of the year for tax purposes.

The time of year you sell should not dominate when you sell. It's best to do it when you're ready and if possible, give yourself as much time as you can.

What about price trends, interest rates, and the economy in general?

These factors usually won't have a bearing on when you list your home for sale. When interest rates are low, there are likely to be more potential buyers who want to take advantage of the low rates. When inventory is tight, it benefits the seller. Your ultimate decision should be guided by your family's needs.

What if I don't have money to invest into a renovation?

Not to worry. We often help sellers prepare to sell their home in as-is condition. As-is condition means selling the property in its current condition. Not all agents can sell homes in as-is condition. This too takes a certain skill set in marketing and negotiations. Be sure to ask your agent if they have sold homes like this before. If they haven't, continue to interview. If they say they have experience, check past clients with whom they sold in as-is.

Does the name and size of the real estate company matter?

The answer is simple - NO.

———

"The biggest myth in the real estate industry is that the name or size of the company matters. The name or size does not negotiate, price, market or communicate.
The agent you choose does."

– John Salkowski

———————

If you're getting ready to sell your home, one of the first questions you might have is how to choose a real estate company to assist you in selling your home.

This is very important.

You are not hiring the real estate company to sell your home. You are hiring the individual real estate professional.

The name or size of the brokerage is a farce and I want to warn you that if any agent tells you this, it is a blatant lie and you should immediately question their integrity. The larger companies who claim to spend the most on marketing or advertising are the very companies who are corporate ran and are very inflexible with creating a personal strategy that works for the seller's independent needs.

The larger companies believe in a one-size-fits-all client system and this just isn't true. The brokerage name on the sign means nothing. It all has to do with what your intuition is telling you about the real estate professional you are interviewing, as well as their track record and systems.

I have held my license at some of the largest companies in the business and I will tell you they collect most of the Realtor's commission so they can pay for the multi-level management system they have in place. You want to hire a realtor that can answer your questions on their own or solve a problem without having to go to their manager for answers.

As I mentioned previously, you want a problem-solver not a messenger. As you may be aware, problem solvers are the most successful business people there are. Messengers merely get by, if at all and end up working for the problem solver. You also want a real estate broker, not just a real estate agent.

WARNING: One more time. The name or size of the brokerage is a farce and I want to warn you that if any agent tells you this, it is a blatant lie and you should immediately question their integrity. If they are telling you this, it's for a reason. That reason being they do not have the confidence in themselves and they need a brand behind them.

The brand DOES NOT negotiate, price, market or communicate. The agent you choose does.

ALWAYS: Request a list of references and call them. Check their online reviews on Zillow.com.

You can always take a peek at ours at **www.JRSRavingReviews.com.**

PART TWO

MONEY TALKS

IT REALLY DOES

How Important Is Pricing Your Home?

In today's market, where demand is outpacing supply in many regions of the country, pricing a house is one of the biggest challenges real estate professionals face. Sellers often want to price their home higher than recommended and many agents go along with the idea just to keep their clients happy. However, an experienced full-time broker realizes that telling the homeowner the truth is more important than getting the seller to like them.

"I can always lower the price ..."

Sellers sometimes think, "If the home doesn't sell for this price, I can always lower it later." However, research proves that homes that experience a listing price reduction sit on the market longer, ultimately selling for less than similar homes.

John Knight, recipient of the University Distinguished Faculty Award from the *Eberhardt School of Business* at the *University of the Pacific*, actually did research on the cost (in both time and money) to a seller who priced high at the beginning and then lowered their price.

In his article, **Listing Price, Time on Market and Ultimate Selling Price** published in *Real Estate Economics* revealed:

"Homes that underwent a price revision sold for less, and the greater the revision, the lower the selling price. Also, the longer the home remains on the market, the lower its ultimate selling price."

Additionally, the "I'll lower the price later" approach can paint a negative image in buyers' minds. Each time a price reduction occurs, buyers can naturally think, "Something must be wrong with that house." Then when a buyer does make an offer, they low-ball the price because they see the seller as "highly motivated." Pricing it right from the start eliminates these challenges.

Don't build "negotiation room" into the price

Many sellers say that they want to price their home high in order to have "negotiation room." But, what this actually does is lower the number of potential buyers that see the house. And we know that limiting demand like this will negatively impact the sales price of the house.

Not sure about this? Think of it this way: when a buyer is looking for a home online (as they do 99 percent of the time), they put in their desired price range. If your seller is looking to sell their house for $400,000, but lists it at $425,000 to build in "negotiation room," any potential buyers that search in the $350k-$400k range won't even know your listing is available, let alone come see it!

A better strategy would be to price it properly from the beginning and bring in multiple offers. This forces these buyers to compete against each other for the "right" to purchase your house.

Look at it this way. If you only receive one offer, you are set up in an adversarial position against the prospective buyer. If, however, you have multiple offers, you have two or more buyers fighting to please you. Which will result in a better selling situation?

Pricing it right the first time

Great pricing comes down to truly understanding the real estate dynamics in your neighborhood. An experienced professional broker will take the time to simply and effectively explain what is happening in the housing market and how it applies to your home. You need a broker that will tell you what you need to know rather than what you want to hear. This will put you in the best possible position.

Things to ... consider:

- **Consider comparables**. What have other homes in your neighborhood sold for recently? How do they compare to yours in terms of size, upkeep, and amenities?
- **Consider competition**. How many other houses are for sale in your area? Are you competing against new homes?
- **Consider your contingencies.** Do you have special concerns that would affect the price you'll receive? For example, do you want to be able to move in four months?
- **Get an appraisal**. For a few hundred dollars, a qualified appraiser can give you an estimate of your home's value. Be sure to ask for a market-value appraisal.
- **Ask a lender**. Since most buyers will need a mortgage, it's important that a home's sale price be in line with a lender's estimate of its value.
- **Be accurate.** Studies show that homes priced more than 3 percent over the correct price take longer to sell.

- **Know what you'll take**. It's critical to know what price you'll accept before beginning a negotiation with a buyer.
- **Don't listen to Zillow**. Zillow promotes Zestimates and so many consumers think this is good information to receive what their property is worth. Zillow is appearing as the authority on pricing homes. How accurate and misleading is the site? The wording from their own company states the following: **"The Zestimate® home valuation is Zillow's estimated market value computed using a proprietary formula. It is not an appraisal. It is a starting point in determining a home's value."** What is the formula used to calculate these numbers? They go on to say that the data is collected from public or user submitted data and real estate agents. Again, this is from their website - We encourage buyers, sellers, and homeowners to supplement Zillow's information by doing other research such as:
- Getting a comparative market analysis (CMA) from a real estate agent
- Getting an appraisal from a professional appraiser
- Visiting the house (whenever possible)

PART THREE

GETTIN' READY

TIPS TO SPRUCE, STAGE ... AND SELL!

"If you follow our proven strategic plan of the industry's best-kept secrets, your home will sell faster and for top dollar. Guaranteed."

– John Salkowski

Our Selling Secrets

Selling Secret #1: Pricing it Right

Find out what your home is worth by an expert, and then shave a small percentage off the price. You'll be stampeded by buyers with multiple bids, even in the worst of markets and they'll bid up the price over what it's worth. It takes real courage and most sellers just don't want to risk it, but it's the single best strategy to sell a home in today's market.

Selling Secret #2: Organize Closets & Keep Them Half-Empty

Storage space is a huge selling point, and if your closets are stuffed to the brim, buyers will think you don't have enough of it. Invest in some boxes, dividers, and other solutions that will help you organize your space, and remove items you don't need (you can stow them away until you move). Buyers will snoop, so be sure to keep all your closets and cabinets clean and tidy.

Selling Secret #3: Light it Up

Maximize the light in your home. After location, good light is the one thing that every buyer cites that they want in a home. Take down the drapes, clean the windows, change the lampshades, increase the wattage of your light bulbs and cut the bushes outside to let in sunshine. Do what you have to do to make your house bright and cheery. It will make it more sellable.

Selling Secret #4: Hire Someone You Trust

Hire a broker you can trust. Call their references. Hire a broker who sells more than 30 homes a year. Make sure you have a broker who is totally informed. They must constantly monitor the Multiple Listing Services (MLS), know what properties are going on the market and know the comps in your neighborhood. Find a tech-savvy broker who embraces technology. One who has the latest tools to get your house sold.

Selling Secret #5: Conceal Your Pets

You might think a cuddly dog would warm the hearts of potential buyers, but you'd be wrong. Not everybody is a dog- or cat-lover. Buyers don't want to walk in your home and see a bowl full of dog food, smell the kitty litter box or have tufts of pet hair stuck to their clothes. It will give buyers the impression that your house is not clean. If you're planning an open house, send the critters to a pet hotel for the day.

Selling Secret #6: Don't Over-Upgrade

Quick fixes before selling always pay off. However, mammoth makeovers? Not so much. You probably won't get your money back if you do a huge improvement project before you put your house on the market. Instead, do updates that will pay off and get you top dollar. Get a new fresh coat of paint on the walls. Clean the curtains or go buy some inexpensive new ones. Replace door handles, cabinet hardware, make sure closet doors are on track, fix leaky faucets and clean the grout.

Selling Secret #7: Take the Home Out of Your House

One of the most important things to do when selling your house is to de-personalize it. The more personal stuff in your house, the less potential buyers can imagine themselves living there. Get rid of a third of your stuff, put it in storage. This includes family photos, memorabilia collections and personal keepsakes. Consider hiring a home stager to maximize the full potential of your home. Staging simply means arranging your furniture to best showcase the floor plan and maximize the use of space.

Selling Secret #8: The Kitchen Comes First

You're not actually selling your house; you're selling your kitchen – that's how important it is. The benefits of remodeling your kitchen are endless, and the best part of it is that you'll probably get 85 percent of your money back. It may be a few thousand dollars to replace counter tops where a buyer may knock $10,000 off the asking price if your kitchen looks dated. The fastest, most inexpensive kitchen updates include painting and new cabinet hardware. Use neutral-color paint so you can present buyers with a blank canvas where they can start envisioning their own style. If you have a little money to spend, buy one fancy stainless steel appliance. Why one? Because when people see one high-end appliance they think all the rest are expensive too and it updates the kitchen.

What Happens at the Curb ... Matters

DID YOU KNOW ... ?
76 percent of home buyers drive by the home they purchase?

They want property information at the curb.
And they want it on their mobile phones.

What happens at the curb... matters.

76% of home buyers drive by the home they purchase. They want property info at the curb. And they want it on their mobile phones.

Our company has invested in VoicePad, the real estate industry's most powerful lead-generating mobile technology... *and it all starts at the curb with the 'smart sign.'*

(555) 555-5555
INFO 24-7 ENTER **8 1 0 0** to
Se Habla Español

PROPERTY INFO
324 STATE STREET

VoicePad mobile technology:
- **Delivers automated property info** to home buyers 24-7 by **Call** and by **Text,** and offers links to your property's **Web Page.** And it works on *any* phone!
- **Captures the identity** of every potential buyer who inquires about your property and **delivers it in real time** to your agent.

Potential buyers call or text for property info and can link to your agent's mobile web page instantly.

You won't find a lead-generating solution like this anywhere else!

On average, 20 percent of callers will instantly connect to your agent for more information. And these are motivated buyers!

DID YOU KNOW ... 55 percent of home buyers found the property they bought from a yard sign.

Selling Secret #9: Always Be Ready to Show

Your house needs to be "show-ready" at all times – you never know when your buyer is going to walk through the door. You have to be available whenever they want to come see the place and it has to be in tip-top shape. Don't leave dishes in the sink, keep the dishwasher cleaned out, bathrooms must sparkle, lower the toilet seat and make sure there are no dust bunnies in the corners of the rooms. It's a little inconvenient, but it will get your house sold.

Selling Secret #10: Clean, Clean, Clean & Clear Out the Clutter

Be sure to clean every nook and cranny. Don't forget overlooked areas, such as dusting the fireplace mantel and ceiling fan blades, polishing appliances and faucets, and washing the windows. If you've already moved out or if you're too busy to do a thorough cleaning, consider hiring a cleaning service. You want buyers to focus on how awesome your space is, not how cluttered it is. Banish that pile of shoes from the entry, that stack of mail from the kitchen table, and anything else that detracts from your home's gorgeous features.

Selling Secret #11: Pay Attention to Odors

Don't cook bacon or anything else that will leave an odor in your home the day of a showing. You don't want your home to smell like a restaurant.

Selling Secret #12: Repaint the Walls in Neutral Colors

As much as you love your different color rooms it could turn off a good portion of your potential buyers. You should repaint in neutral tones such as grays, tans, and whites that allow buyers to focus on the spaces, not the color of the walls.

Selling Secret #13: Keep the Decor Simple.

To help buyers imagine themselves in your space, get rid of any statement art or decor that might turn people off. A classic landscape painting is totally fine, however your zebra-print leather couch? You may want to place a slip-cover over that for showings or rent a storage unit until you're ready to move it into your new place.

Selling Secret #14: Bring Nature Inside

Potted plants or a few pretty buds in a vase can help bring energy into a space, fill in empty corners, and even draw attention to features you want buyers to notice. Just make sure the plants are in good health.

Selling Secret #15: Get Rid of Bulky Furniture

Your furniture should fit the scale of the room, so get rid of any extra or oversized items that could make your space look smaller than it really is. For example, if you have a huge sectional in your family room, consider breaking it up and just use the main sofa portion.

Selling Secret #16: Give Each Room a Purpose

That spare room you've been using as an office/guest room/dumping ground won't help sell your home unless you show buyers how they can use it themselves. So pick a use (office, guest room, crafts room) and clearly stage the space to showcase that purpose.

Selling Secret #17: Turn the Bathroom into a Spa

Create the feel of a relaxing, luxurious bath -- for less than $30. Stack a few pretty washcloths tied with ribbon, add some candles and orchids, and buy bathmats and towels in coordinating tones such as light green, blue, and white.

Selling Secret #18: Turn the Living Room into Conversation Central

Practice the art of Feng Shui. Help buyers picture themselves relaxing with family and guests by grouping your furniture into arrangements that inspire conversation.

Selling Secret #19: Keep the Flow Going

The last thing you want is people bumping into furniture as they tour your home. It disrupts their focus and makes your space look cramped. Do a dry run as though you're seeing your home for the first time and tweak anything that interrupts the "flow."

Selling Secret #20: Make Something Yummy

Real estate agents don't put out fresh cookies at open houses just to treat buyers. A "homey" smell such as cookies or muffins baking can help people connect with a kitchen. Not a baker? Fake it with a scented candle.

Selling Secret #21: Make it Look Lived in With Vignettes

Help your buyers see themselves in your home by adding deliberate vignettes that showcase how your home can be lived in. An inviting armchair and a tray with a coffee cup and book on it can turn that empty corner into a reading nook. Pretty soaps in a decorative tray can make your tiny half bath more appealing.

Selling Secret #22: Highlight Focal Points.

Draw buyers' eyes toward any special features with bright colors or accents such as plants. A pop of red from a throw pillow can draw buyers' attention to that lovely window seat. A striking fern on the mantel can show off your fireplace.

Selling Secret #23: The First Impression is the Only Impression

No matter how good the interior of your home looks, buyers have already judged your home before they walk through the door. You never have a second chance to make a first impression.

Boost your curb appeal. Don't spend all your time indoors. Buyers may decide to not enter a home based on its curb appeal, so make sure your home's exterior looks excellent. Trim shrubs, weed flowerbeds, remove and refresh any peeling paint, and keep the walkway clear. Just adding a row of potted plants along the walkway or a cheerful wreath to your front door can make a big difference. We recommend that you focus on curb appeal first. On a tight budget, then we advise that you at least spruce up the front entrance.

Do's and Don'ts of Over-Improving Your Home

Every homeowner who has contemplated a home improvement project has wondered how much the project would add to the value of his or her home. It's almost never a question of, "Will it?" It's always, "How much?"

The good news is that according to the most recent Cost vs. Value report from Remodeling.com, most home improvement projects will add some value to your home. But - and this is an important *but* - your project probably won't boost your home's value enough to recoup the entire cost of the improvement. And in some cases, your upgrade may not add any value to your home at all.

We've categorized these home improvements in to four types:

- Improvements to avoid if you plan to sell your home
- Improvements to make if you plan to stay in your home
- Improvements to make if you plan to sell your home
- Invisible improvements

Improvements to Avoid if You Plan to Sell Your Home

The return on investment (ROI) on some projects is so low; you'll be left holding the bag for about half the cost. That makes these especially poor choices for homeowners planning to sell.

- Sunroom addition: Cost–$75,700, ROI–48%
- Home office remodel: Cost–$29,000, ROI–48%
- Bathroom addition: Cost–$40,000, ROI–57%

These improvements aren't *always* bad choices. If you'll be living in your home a while and would enjoy a sunroom, extra bathroom or home office, go for it! But **think twice (or a few more times) before you take on any of these projects** solely for the purpose of increasing the sales value of your home.

Improvements to Make if You Plan to Stay in Your Home

In general, projects that add square-footage are best viewed as an investment in your family's enjoyment of your home. At most, you can expect to recover just 64% of the cost of a family room, garage or second-story addition - even less for sunrooms and bathrooms.

You'll do a little better converting unused area like your attic or basement in to living spaces. An attic bedroom will return 77% of its $51,000 price tag, and a $17,000 basement renovation will recoup 70 cents for every dollar you spend.

If you're planning to stay in your home a few more years and need the extra space to keep family members from tripping over each other, by all means add the space! Your family will have plenty of time to appreciate the addition and, once you're ready to sell, the boost in square footage will also boost your asking price.

Improvements to Make if You Plan to Sell

As we pointed out, large-scale projects don't usually translate into large increases in your home's value. So, when you're ready to sell, upgrades that make an impact for less money are the way to go.

For the last several years, **simply replacing your front door with a new steel entry door has had the best ROI.** According to the Cost vs. Value report, this is the one project that will pay for itself, returning nearly 102% of its $1,200 cost.

Other projects that improve your home's curb appeal are also good bets:

- Replace vinyl siding with manufactured stone veneer accents: Cost–$7,150, ROI–92%
- Garage door replacement: Cost–$1,595, ROI–88%
- Replace vinyl siding: Cost–$12,000, ROI–80%
- Wood deck addition: Cost–$10,000, ROI–80%

Inside, a minor kitchen remodel will earn back 79% of its $19,000 cost. That includes replacing outdated appliances, re-facing the cabinets and adding new hardware, updating the laminate countertop and sink and replacing the flooring.

Invisible Improvements

You can drop a huge chunk of cash on home maintenance projects like replacing your heating and cooling unit, hot water heater or even your septic system. Unfortunately, even when these updates are brand new, most buyers aren't willing to pay more for them. Buyers expect functional features like these to simply function, and they don't feel like they should pay for wear and tear that occurred in the home while you owned it.

On the other hand, **if any of these invisible parts of your home aren't in working order, it will detract big time from your home's**

value. Even if you plan to sell soon, you can't avoid these problems since they will certainly turn up in a home inspection. Go ahead and tackle the problems, just realize you're *maintaining* your home's value - not adding to it.

However, one update most homeowners would consider a maintenance project falls into a gray area of home improvement: a roof replacement. A new roof certainly isn't a showpiece like a top-to-bottom kitchen renovation, but according to Remodeling.com, it can boost your home's value. On average, homeowners nationwide can expect to recoup more than 70 percent of the $20,000 price tag of a mid-range roof replacement project.

Preparing Your Home For Photography

At The JRS Realty Group, our #1 goal is to present your home at its best. Your goal should be to present a clean, spacious, clutter-free home – the kind you'd like to buy! Photographs could possibly make or break the sale of your home, since the first impression is online so we've created a checklist to help you prepare your home for photos:

Curb Appeal:
- Mow lawn and trim shrubs
- Edge gardens and walkways
- Remove all cars from driveway
- Hide garbage cans inside garage
- Sweep walkways and driveways, remove branches, litter, and toys
- Add color and fill bare spots with plantings
- Remove mildew or moss from walls or walks with bleach and water
- Take stains off your driveway with cleaner or kitty litter
- Stack woodpile neatly
- Clean and repair patio and deck areas
- Remove any outdoor furniture that is not in good shape
- Make sure pool is sparkling clean
- Replace old storm doors
- Check for flat-fitting roof shingles
- Repair broken windows/shutters, replace torn screens, make sure frames and seams have solid caulking
- Hose off exterior wood and trim, replace damaged bricks or wood

- Clean/remove rust from any window A/C units or store them away
- Paint the front door and mailbox
- Add a new front door mat and consider seasonal door decoration
- Shine brass hardware on front door, exterior lighting fixtures, etc.
- Make sure doorbell is in working order

General Interior Tips:

- Add a fresh coat of interior paint in light, neutral colors
- Shampoo carpeting, replace if necessary
- Clean and wax hardwood floors, refinish if necessary
- Clean and wash kitchen and bathroom floors
- Wash all windows, vacuum blinds, wash window sills
- Clean the fireplace
- Clean out and organize closets, add extra space by packing clothes and items you won't need again until after you've moved
- Remove extra furniture, worn rugs, and items you don't use: put away papers, toys, etc., especially from stairs
- Repair easy fixes: loose doorknobs, cracked molding, leaky taps and toilets, squeaky doors, closet or screen doors off their tracks, etc.
- Add dished potpourri or drop of vanilla or bath oil on light bulbs for scent
- Secure jewelry, cash, or other valuables

Kitchen:

- Make sure appliances are spotless inside and out (try baking soda for cleaning Formica stains)
- Make sure all appliances are in working order
- Clean often-forgotten spots on top of fridge and under sink
- Wax or sponge floors to brilliant shine, clean baseboards
- Organize items inside cabinets, pre-pack anything you won't be using before your move
- Keep counters as clear and empty as possible

Living Room:

- Make it cozy and inviting, discard chipped or worn furniture and frayed or worn rugs
- Consider packing away personal photos

- Remove as much clutter as possible

Bathrooms:
- Remove all rust and mildew
- Make sure tile, fixtures, shower doors, are immaculate and shining
- Stow all personal hygiene items
- Put out fresh towels and linens

Master Bedroom:
- Organize furniture to create a spacious look with well-defined sitting, sleeping, and dressing areas
- Organize and minimize clutter in closets

Dining Room:
- Polish any visible silver or crystal
- Set the table for a formal dinner to help viewers imagine entertaining here

Basement:
- Sell, give away, or throw out all unnecessary items
- Organize and create more space by hanging tools and placing items on shelves
- Clean water heater and drain sediment
- Change furnace filter
- Make inspection access easy
- Clean and paint concrete floors and walls
- Provide strong overhead lighting

Attic:
- Tidy up by discarding or pre-packing
- Make sure exposed insulation is visible and in good condition
- Make sure air vent is in good working order
- Provide strong overhead lighting

Must-Do's Before Showing Your Home

The "For Sale" sign is up. You've completed the necessary projects and made the little tweaks, hopeful your efforts will pay off with a quick, full price offer. But now comes the most critical part of the home-selling cycle -

the day of a showing or an open house. A negative first impression can directly affect an offer at full asking price. Before opening the door to potential buyers, the day of a showing, we highly suggest you follow these tips.

1. **Detach from the stuff**. Home staging experts agree the first and most important step to a successful listing is to emotionally separate from the house and the objects within it. Many clients we work with battle to let go of their property and refuse to take down family photographs and religious items. Letting go of the emotional connections to the items inside the home will make you more objective about any necessary changes and more open to Realtor and buyer feedback. To ease the selling process, embrace the idea that your house is a commodity that needs to be sold, and transfer any emotional connections to your new home.

Don't forget: Foyer tables, fireplace mantels and refrigerator doors are popular display spots for loads of personal items like holiday cards, children's artwork, pictures and trophies. Pare down or clear off these spots for showings.

2. **Make sure it looks clean.** Cleaning seems so obvious, and is inexpensive, but the lack of it is one of the biggest complaints real estate agents hear. Hopefully, you've done the big scrub leading up to open-house day: carpets steamed, floors mopped, windows wiped, appliances scoured. But on the day of a showing, don't overlook little details like crumbs on the table from breakfast, toothpaste remnants in sinks, half-full trash cans on display and dust bunnies in rooms you don't frequent. Do a quick walk-through with a duster, reaching into recessed lights and corners. Straighten the bedspreads in all the rooms, put away shoes in hallways and tuck away pet beds and food, water bowls.

Don't forget: Wipe down surfaces that people would naturally touch, such as stair banisters, handrails and items that have inviting textures. People love touching things. Textures change everything and scream "touch me" as they propel people into various good spots in their memories.

3. **Make sure it smells clean.** Besides a home's visual appeal, nothing triggers more comments than odors. Diffuse cooking, pet and musty odors by airing out the home with open windows or air purifiers. Comforting smells, like baking bread or brewing coffee, can be appealing to most potential buyers. We always recommend fresh flowers, burning a nice candle or boil some apples and lemons before you leave the house.

However, be careful with too many scents, such as strong spray scents, candles or other products. Don't leave plug-in air fresheners around your home. Some people are allergic to scents, and it only highlights that you have an odor or dampness problem.

Don't forget: Pet foods, toys, litter boxes and blankets may have distinct smells. Stow these items or take them out of the house during showings.

4. Remove sight-line clutter. Eliminate items such as knick-knacks; toys, small appliances and bath products that stop the eye, or worse, make spaces look smaller. You are selling the space and finishes of the house, not your personal property. Always be mindful of this. Though many rugs add warmth and color, consider rolling them up if they break up a room disjointedly or if they obscure attractive selling points like stunning hardwood floors or beautiful tilework. Bathrooms, especially small ones, will look bigger without the rugs. If it's a huge master bath with a coordinated rug, then it may stay if it warms up a big, cold space. Have bins or baskets on hand to clear off countertops, floors, tables and desks.

Don't forget: Store tablecloths and dish towels to accentuate a kitchen's workspace and appliances. Kitchens look larger if your eye does not stop at the dishtowel on the oven, dishwasher and sink.

5. Improve traffic flow. Over time, homeowners become desensitized to what their possessions look like and where they are placed. The coat rack or shoe rack by the front door might be practical for your family, but it can look like poor storage to a potential buyer. Walk through each room and determine if the furniture arrangement contributes to a comfortable flow and use of space.

Don't forget: Too little furniture can be just as bad as too much. A tiny couch in a large family room might prompt buyers to worry they'll never be able to furnish the whole space. If needed, re-purpose pieces from spare rooms to comfortably fill out an area.

6. Create the "Goldilocks Effect." No matter what time of day or year, the home's temperature, lighting and noise levels should be just right during a showing. Room temperatures should be not too hot and not too cold. Blinds, shades and drapes should be open and of equal length/height, and lights should be on. A dark house will turn potential buyers off for sure.

Don't forget: Let in pleasant ambient sounds, from birds chirping outside to a soothing water feature. Calming music in the background, high enough to hear but low enough to not overwhelm, will do wonders.

When It's Time to Show:

- Make sure all marketing materials are readily available in a convenient location, such as the kitchen
- Open all draperies and shades, turn on all lights
- Keep the home at a comfortable temperature
- Pick up toys and other clutter, check to make sure beds are made and clothes are put away
- Give the carpets a quick vacuuming
- Avoid using the dishwasher, washer, and dryer while your home is being shown
- Add some strategically placed fresh flowers throughout the home
- Open bathroom window for fresh air
- Store prescription drugs in a private place
- Pop a spicy dessert or just a pan of cinnamon in the oven for aroma. The smell of freshly-baked cookies is always appealing.
- Grind fresh lemon in the garbage disposal or boil cinnamon sticks to add a fresh scent
- Turn of the TV and put on some light, non-offensive music at a low volume
- Make a fire in the fireplace (optional)
- Put pets in the backyard or arrange for a friend to keep them
- Make sure pet areas are clean and 100% odor-free

Why a Pre-Sale Home Inspection is an Investment – Not an Expense

———

"Anticipating any problems and staying proactive, the home inspector or buyer may have with your home — and fixing these problems — will save you money."
– John Salkowski

———

1 - <u>You'll have to fix problems anyway or make concessions</u>

Your buyers are going to do a home inspection, and the inspector will be able to identify all the issues and suggest needed repairs. There's no avoiding it. You *will* have to fix any problems, credit money back to the buyer, or drop your price to compensate.

2 - <u>It will save you money</u>

Many repairs are easy to solve, inexpensive, and can be tackled in a weekend. They're likely to be the things that were already on your list of weekend projects for the past year, and if they bother you, they'll also bother a buyer. Leaky faucets, ripped window screens, ceiling stains, cracks in the plaster, they may seem like minor issues, but when you've got a whole house full of problems like these, they add up to one big seller headache.

3 - <u>Your home - Not its flaws will be the focus</u>

Eliminating distracting drawbacks will allow buyers to have a positive experience as they tour your home. That means buyers viewing your home will be able to focus on your home's positive, not negative, features.

4 - <u>A well-maintained home gets better offers</u>

Getting your home completely prepped and ready will increase its "Perceived Value" because you're showing buyers that your property is well maintained.

5 - <u>You can hold firm on your price</u>

You won't have to do a price reduction to reflect the estimated (and often overinflated) cost of repairs.

6 - <u>Rush jobs cost more, every time</u>

Last-minute repairs done on a tight timeline are almost always costlier since you don't have time to shop around for estimates. Plus, your time crunch begs for tradespeople to charge higher rush fees for squeezing the work into their schedule.

7 - <u>Actual costs and estimates don't always match</u>

Your actual cost to fix an item will almost always be less than a buyer's estimate after their inspection — but since you won't necessarily have time to fix everything before closing, you risk losing the sale if you don't agree to the estimate.

8 - <u>You won't risk losing the deal</u>

You'll avoid credits back to the buyer for problems identified during the inspection and haggling that drags on and on over minor issues, possibly costing you the deal. (You'd be surprised how ugly things can get when you're down to the wire negotiating the added cost of repairing the cracks in the chimney.)

9 - <u>You'll get more potential buyers in the door</u>

Realtors love showing an impeccable home, and their buyer clients will be dying to get in the front door. That brings in more potential buyers — which equates to more chances of finding the right one willing to pay your sale price.

10 - <u>You'll sell your home faster - and for a higher price</u>

Having pre-sale home inspection(s): septic, well, termite, radon, stucco is one of the smartest things you can do before selling your home. I highly urge all sellers to take advantage of a pre-sale inspection before showings get under way. This way you know what you're up against in terms of repairs and can get them taken care of before any potential buyers see your home.

Smart sellers choose not to skip an early inspection. I make these inspections available to my clients at a reduced price. Sellers have found out that this can save them thousands of dollars in the long run and just as important, it eliminates the need for back-end negotiations, which can be a deal-killer.

At this point in the process, it has found to be the most stressful part of the transaction. Buyers love the pre-sale home inspection as well, because it shows the seller is pre-certifying their home. This ultimately increases the buyer's confidence. This will not, in most cases, take the place of the buyer's doing their own inspection. However it makes you, the seller, aware what needs to be addressed or not addressed and most importantly what could kill a deal before the buyers see your home, places their offer and ultimately, having their own inspection.

PART FOUR

MARKETING

TIME TO GO TO WORK!

Important Reasons to Hire a Real Estate Professional

With more than 13 million homes being sold across the country each year and the increasing number of short sales and foreclosures, the process of selling a home has become more complex than ever. The paperwork is lengthy, tedious and confusing if not prepared properly, may cause a severe liability issues. It certainly can be difficult to navigate alone. You'll undoubtedly benefit from the services of an experienced, full-time professional real estate broker on your side. The distinct advantages of entrusting the services of a real estate broker include:

- **Marketing** – As I've always said, real estate brokers are in the business of marketing their real estate services first, the home selling business second. You must reach and capture the attention of the consumers interested in buying a home. With the right broker, they will showcase your property to other real estate agents and the public. Your agent provides relevant information about your home through a multiple listing service (MLS), which then syndicates to a myriad of online tools and portals.

- **Security** – Take the advice from a retired police officer. Not everyone is honest and trustworthy. When you hire a real estate broker, you don't have to worry about letting strangers into your home alone. Instead, the buyers must be accompanied by a real estate professional. This reduces safety and liability issues.

Negotiation – Having a broker help you evaluate offers and guide you through confusing appraisals, inspections, and financing issues that may arise. Negotiation is a skill set. It's a learnable skill, however; you must approach each and every phase of a deal as a win-win. Without a win-win, everyone loses.

- **Closing Process** – The **closing**, or **settlement** process itself general takes place at one table (either at the office of an attorney, title company or brokers office), where buyers sign all documents related to their loan and the transaction itself. After all documents are signed and payments exchanged, the deed is recorded with the county. Buyers generally take possession of the keys immediately thereafter, unless a separate agreement has been reached to allow the seller to stay in the property for a period after closing.

The detailed steps that make up closing are:

1. As part of the preparation for closing, the attorney or title company performs a **title search** (if they haven't already) to determine if there are any liens or assessments on the title. Provided the title is deemed 'clear,' the closing proceeds as planned and the attorney or title company issues a **title commitment**. All paperwork for changing the title / deed and **title insurance** is prepared, and a final **closing date** is confirmed with all parties.

- **Real Estate Technology** – An experienced full-time professional real estate broker uses cutting edge real estate technology. By definition, Real Estate Tech refers to innovative technological approach that empowers the people in the real estate industry, including agents and brokers.

- **Market Snapshots** – Your broker can easily notify you with updates on new-home listings, pending or under contract homes sales, homes that have sold or not, and homes that have been removed from the market via expired, withdrawn.

Not All Real Estate Agents Are The Same

"It's critical that you make the right decision about who will handle what is probably the single largest financial and emotional investment you will ever make."

– John Salkowski

Not all real estate agents are the same. Not all physicians, attorneys, accountants, financial advisors are the same either. If you decide to seek the help of an agent when selling or buying your home, you need some good information before you make any moves.

An agent can cost OR save you thousands of dollars

Picking a broker is one of those critical issues that can cost or save you thousands of dollars. There are very specific questions you should be asking to ensure that you get the best representation for your needs. Some brokers may
prefer that you don't ask these questions, because the knowledge you'll gain from their honest answers will give you a very good idea about what outcome you can expect from using them. Let's face it - in real estate, as in life - not all things are created equal. Hiring a real estate broker is just like any hiring process - with you on the boss's side of the desk. It's critical that you make the right decision about who will handle what is probably the single largest financial and emotional investment you will ever make.

What makes you different? Why should I sell my home with you?

It's a much tougher real estate market than it was a decade ago. What unique marketing plans and programs does this broker have in place to make sure that your home stands out favorably versus other competing homes? What things does this broker offer you that others don't to help you sell your home in the least amount of time with the least amount of hassle and for the most amount of money?

Scheduling Appointments Was Never So Easy!

We utilize all the cutting-edge technology, systems and services for our clients. Our staff at ShowingTime™ facilitates each and every appointment for your home, seven days a week, 365-days-a-year. They're available Monday through Friday, 8 a.m. to 8 p.m., and Saturday and Sunday from 8 a.m. to 6 p.m. Realtors can schedule a showing on your home via online and/or phone. It is the best way to schedule a showing on your home so nothing gets missed or overlooked.

What is your company's track record and reputation in the market place?

It may seem like everywhere you look, real estate brokers are boasting about themselves, how great they are, about being "#1" for this or that, or quoting you the number of homes they've sold.

If you're like many homeowners, you've probably become immune to much of this babble. After all, you ask, "*Why should I care about how many homes one agent sold over another. The only thing I care about is whether they can sell my home quickly for the most amount of money.*"

Well, because you want your home sold fast and for top dollar, you **SHOULD** be asking the agents you interview how many homes they have sold. I'm sure you will agree that success leaves clues and in real estate it is selling homes. If one agent is selling a lot of homes where another is selling only a few, ask yourself why this might be.

What things are these two agents doing differently? You may be surprised to know that many agents sell fewer than 6 homes a year. This volume makes it difficult for them to do full impact marketing on your home, because they can't raise the money it takes to afford the marketing and special programs to give your home a high profile. Also, at this low level, they probably can't afford to hire an assistant, which means that they're running around trying to do all the components of the job themselves, which means their service may suffer.

What are your marketing plans for my home?

How much money does this agent spend in advertising the homes he or she lists versus the other agents you are interviewing? In what media (online, magazine, radio etc.) does this agent advertise? What does she or he know about the effectiveness of one medium over the other?

What has your company sold in my area?

Agents should bring you a complete listing of both their own, and other comparable sales in your area.

What Happens on Social Media Matters

What happens on
social media...
matters.

Adults today spend 28% of their time online on social networks. Today it is essential to market properties via social media.

Your Agent has invested in VoicePad,® an **Automated Property Marketing system to maximize your home's online exposure**...*and it includes social media!*

Social Media content is automatically created to showcase your home by incorporating listing data and photos. Posts, Tweets and Ads can be published for;

- **New Listing**
- **Open House**
- **Price Updates**
- **And more!**

Social Listing Tool 9/2015

Adults today spend 28% of their time online on social networks.
Today it is essential to market properties via social media.
Agents should bring you a complete listing of both their own, and other comparable sales in your area.

Does your broker control your marketing or do YOU?

If your agent is not in control of their own marketing, then your home will be competing for advertising space not only with this agent's other listings, but also with the listings of every other agent in the brokerage.

On average, when your listings sell, how close is the selling price to the asking price?

This information is available from the MLS – Multiple Listing Service. Is this agent's performance higher or lower than the board average? Their performance on this measurement will help you predict how high a price you will get for the sale of your home.

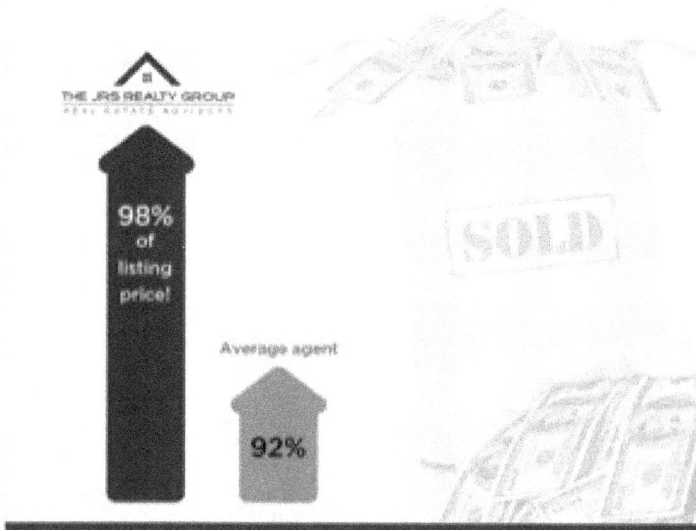

On average, how long does it take for your listings to sell?

This information is also available from the MLS – multiple listing service. Does this agent tend to sell faster or slower than the board average? Their performance on this measurement will help you predict how long your home will be on the market before it sells.

How many buyers are you currently working with?

Obviously, the more buyers your agent is working with, the better your chances are of selling your home quickly. It will also impact price because an agent with many buyers can set up an auction-like atmosphere where many buyers bid on your home at the same time. Ask them to describe the system they have for attracting buyers.

Do you have a reference list of clients I could contact?

Ask to see this list, and then proceed to spot-check some of the names by calling and asking questions.

What happens if I'm NOT happy with the job you are doing to get my home sold? Can I cancel my listing contract?

Be very wary of agents that lock you into a lengthy listing contract which they can get out of (by ceasing to effectively market your home) but you can't. There are usually penalties and broker protection periods which safeguard the agent's interests, but not yours. How confident is your agent in the service s/he will provide you? Will s/he allow you to cancel your contract without penalty if you're not satisfied with the service provided? Evaluate each agent's responses to these 10 questions carefully and objectively. Who will do the best job for you? These questions will help you decide.

Individual Agent vs. Team Structure

————————

"Selling real estate is no different than how a hospital emergency room operates. You have a multitude of people doing certain tasks - from signing you in to taking your vitals to drawing blood to examining you. There is no difference in real estate industry. You do not want one person wearing all the hats. Things are bound to be forgotten."

– John Salkowski

————————

The benefits of our team concept:

- Listing Agent Specialist
- Professional, licensed, full-time Brokers handling the listing of your home.
- Experienced Brokers handle all negotiations
- Upload photos, create virtual tours, make highlight sheets and input listing onto multiple websites and the MLS
- 24-hour recorded message
- Manage marketing programs
- Manage any listing questions and detail Closing Coordinators
- Professional, full-time closing coordinators handling the sale of your home through transfer of title
- Daily contact with Lenders, Title Companies, Inspectors, Agents, Loan Officers, etc.
- Schedule and follow-up with appraisals
- Hand over the keys to the new buyer!
- Lead Management System
- Full-time lead coordinator
- Never miss out on possible buyers
- Get qualified buyers into your home and making offers!
- Ensures buyers are pre-approved for loan

Why You Should Think Again About Selling on Your Own

_____

"Selling your own home can be like performing open heart surgery on yourself - very painful."

– John Salkowski

_____

The leading reason why most homeowners try to sell their home on their own is to save money. Thinking of saving money might sound nice, statistically you'll find that the money you pay for the experience and skills of a professional Real Estate Broker is well worth the investment, not to mention the stress you'll have throughout the process.

Other significant disadvantages:

Lack of Safety

The number one reason NOT to sell on your own - safety. Most FSBOs (For Sale By Owners) do not consider the safety of themselves and their families when allowing strangers into their home to show it. They are often so excited when someone wants to see their home that they just let them right in with no questions asked.

Take it from a retired police officer - thieves and burglars target FSBOs. Prescription drug addicts do as well. What's to stop a thief from waltzing through your house (or two that go in opposite directions) and unlocking a window so they can easily break into your home the same night? What will you do when two people want to see your house together and they split once they're through the door. One heads for the kitchen while the other mysteriously disappears down the hall into every bathroom in your house (checking medicine cabinets for prescription drugs)?

Is it possible that thieves and drug addicts will come through your house with a Realtor? Of course, but it's not as likely. Experienced Realtors know to watch for this sort of behavior and one of the first things a listing agent should point out to the home owner is that they ought to remove all valuables (jewelry, etc.) and prescription drugs from their home during showings and open houses.

Liability

There's a reason Realtors are required to carry (E&O) Error and Omissions insurance. We live in a litigious society.

Lack of Real Estate Knowledge

Do you know the national and state real estate law? Did you know that if you sell a house built before 1978 then you are required to give the buyer a copy of the EPA's report on the dangers of lead paint? Even a FSBO is required to provide that and it's a $10,000+ fine if you neglect to do it.

Lack of interest

Realtors rarely show homes in which a seller is representing themselves. Sellers are generally too emotional to negotiate with. Therefore, they are avoided.

Lack of Pricing Knowledge

Not knowing how much to ask for your home can be a big problem. If you overprice it, which is common among those who try to sell themselves, it won't sell. If you don't ask enough, you'll lose thousands. A Realtor is up-to-date on market conditions and is trained to price your home accurately.

Not knowing what you need to do to show your house. You may make the mistake of over improving/investing too much money into modernizing your house. Conversely, you may neglect to do the simple things that will make your home look its best. A Realtor will guide you in successfully giving you tips on what to do and more importantly not to do in showing your house.

Lack of guidance in creating detailed marketing strategy that suits your specific needs.

Lack of exposure online

There are real estate brokers that will place your home on the MLS for a fee, however that is where it begins and ends. Online is where everyone starts to search for homes.

You will schedule all showings, answer all calls, have unknown, possibly unqualified buyers in your home.

You will be negotiating against yourself. Not to mention the skillset negotiating takes.

"Traditional" Open House? Thumbs Up or Down?

Real estate open houses are one sales tactic that may be more about the hype than about results. Some real estate agents play up the benefits far more than they should, considering how many drawbacks there are to the process. The fact is, open houses are rarely conducted to sell a home. Sure, some agents still believe that the open house has a place in the sale of a home. There will always be home owners that do not know any better. However, the facts about open houses should discourage anyone from bothering with the process.

The debate over whether an open house is a good marketing activity almost always boils down to a battle between real estate agents who are at the pinnacle of their game (top producers) and those agents who need to do open houses to generate additional clients. In other words, real estate open houses can be significant prospecting activities for Realtors. **Do open houses sell homes?** The answer statistically is clear – **Less than 1 percent nationally**!

Some real estate agents have to do open houses, or they wouldn't know where to find their next prospect if it hit them in the face. *What consumers need to understand is that "real buyers" schedule appointments to see homes they are interested in viewing.*

How many buyers who are ready, willing and able to purchase a home say to themselves – if those Realtors don't have an open house – forget about it I'm not interested!" Sounds pretty moronic, doesn't it? That's because it is. When weighing the pros and cons of an open house, the cons come in ahead by a large margin! Open houses rarely work to sell a home and put sellers at undue risk.

Why We Discourage Your Traditional Open House

Security issues – One of the biggest drawbacks of an open house is the potential for theft. Letting strangers in off the street to wander around your home carries some obvious security risks. While the majority of visitors will most likely be there to view your home, and learn more about it, some may be there for more nefarious reasons. The fact is, during an open house anyone can come in – even people who are looking for access points, security weaknesses, and valuables. This is something most real estate agents who tout open houses ever want to discuss. They will sweep this fact right under the rug at the seller's expense just to keep their lead generation train rolling.

The risk of theft – This ties into security issues, but it deserves its own section. There have been documented cases of people breaking into houses for sale and stealing things. Sometimes they do it in unoccupied homes, and sometimes they do it in homes that people are still living in. The temptation is too much – they can walk into the open house, see what they want to take and how they can get in, and then they later burglarize the place. Folks this is not just an isolated example – this happens all around the country! An open house is an open invitation to make theft more probable. If you want to have your broker host an open house then here are my suggestions: Ask for ID of each and every visitor and have them sign in. If they do not have ID then they do not enter. Insist on the broker accompanying the visitors around the house. If there are multiple visitors that are not together, have them wait outside. I know this may sound harsh, however its for your safety.

Unqualified prospects – Have you ever driven through a beautiful neighborhood and seen an open house – a lovely house – and thought about stopping in to check it out? Most people have at least considered it. There is not really anything wrong with doing so – how often do you get the chance to see how other people live and decorate? The problem is, often the people coming into your open house are doing the same thing. Just stopping in to check things out, not to buy. Come on in everybody! As long as you have a heartbeat you are welcome here.

Nosy neighbors – An open house is like a beacon to neighbors curious about your home. They may be great neighbors or not so great neighbors. However good they are to live by, you may not want them wandering around your house. Unfortunately, there is no real way to stop them. Once you open your home, most anyone can walk through the doors. Expect the busy bees stopping by your home to be discussing it with all the rest of the neighbors who failed to show up.

Lack of one-on one-attention – Your Realtor may be motivated to sell your home, but he or she only has the ability to communicate with one set of buyers at a time. This means that if things get busy, there will be a lot of missed opportunities – people that may have been perfect prospective buyers that never even get to speak to the real estate agent. There is no way for an open house visit to compare to an actual home viewing with your agent. Most people who come by and visit are probably going to want to return at a later date to really check things out if they are serious buyers anyways.

Seller competition – Other people selling their homes are likely to stop by and see what you are doing with yours. This only makes sense, especially if they are in a similar neighborhood with a similar home to sell. However, these visitors do you no good. They will simply see what you are doing and take what works for them.

In fact, if they look over your home and think it looks pretty darn good they will probably be dropping the price of their home to be more competitive. This is an excellent example of helping the competition. Most sellers who are competing against you wouldn't schedule a showing to do the same snooping they would do at an open house.

Agent's ulterior motives – Some agents may be excited to do an open house and be firmly convinced that it is a valid sales method. However, a lot of agents use open houses to attract other clients. All of those unwanted visitors – with the exception of the burglars – are potential customers for the agent.

How We Revolutionized the Open House

Instead of doing the failed traditional method of the open house like you read previously, we have revolutionized the open house that works like a charm.

It's called "Everyday Open House, Call for Times." It is a separate standalone sign that we use with a trackable number that is automatically texted and emailed to the agent on rotation when someone calls through our proprietary phone system. Here's how it works:

Since no buyer wants to be sold too and/or talk with a real estate agent, therefore making the for-sale sign virtually useless other than letting the public know that the home is for sale. We utilize a separate sign that sits beside the for-sale sign. This sign gets 100% more calls from potential buyers. They call the sign because it says, everyday open house call for times. The buyer(s) will call and state that they are sitting outside of 123 Main St. and they want to see the house.

At this point, we follow our systemized approach by following our script to qualify them. No buyer enters a home that we have listed without first being pre-approved by a reputable lender. We have sold more of our own listings using this system than any other way, as well as converting more buyers into clients.

Our Concierge Trusted Advisors

My approach to business always starts with this acronym, WIFM – What's in it for me – meaning you my client. In business, as in my personal life, I always approach a relationship from a fiduciary standpoint. Being a fiduciary to others means always putting their interest before my own. I make sure that I put more into a relationship than I expect in return. With this in mind, I want to always add value to others I touch. Therefore, creating a list of trusted advisors to share with my clients. Trusted advisors meaning trusted vendors such as attorney's, financial planners, title company, contractors, mortgage bankers, landscapers, accountants, handymen, electricians, inspectors.

When clients use, my concierge trusted advisors service, they never have to guess if the professional will be able to meet their needs. A member of my firm personally matches every homeowner who calls with the appropriate vendor. Our goal is to build relationships with our clients, therefore creating raving fans as well as being an active part of the community.

Not Your Typical Realtor

Easy Exit Listing Guarantee

Integrity means everything to me.

What's your biggest fear when you list your home with a real estate agent?

It's simple. You worry about being locked into a lengthy listing agreement with a less than competent real estate agent, costing your home valuable time and exposure on the market. Worry no more.

The JRS Realty Group takes the risk and fear out of listing your home with a real estate agent. How?

Through the **One Day Listing Guarantee**.

When you list your home through The JRS Realty Group's One Day Listing Guarantee, you can cancel your listing anytime. You can relax, knowing you won't be locked into a lengthy or binding contract. Enjoy the caliber of service confident enough to make this offer to you. If at any time, you no longer want us to market your property, you may cancel the listing and pay nothing! You do not eve have to give us advanced noticed. Simply pick up the phone, send an email and tell us.

Only two exceptions: This will not apply if active negotiations have started and/or contracts are pending.

Where to turn if your home doesn't sell the first time?

We succeed where others have failed. The numbers don't lie.

JOHN SALKOWSKI - BY THE NUMBERS

NUMBERS DON'T LIE!

CASE #1: 334 SAUNDERS DRIVE
NUMBER OF AGENTS <u>BEFORE JOHN</u>: 1
DAYS ON MARKET <u>BEFORE JOHN</u>: 185
WITH JOHN: SOLD – 4 DAYS – 95% Asking Price

CASE #2: 1209 N. CHARLOTTE STREET
NUMBER OF AGENTS <u>BEFORE JOHN</u>: 1
DAYS ON MARKET <u>BEFORE JOHN</u>: 131
WITH JOHN: SOLD – 18 DAYS – 97% Asking Price

CASE #3: 2647 N. CHARLOTTE STREET
NUMBER OF AGENTS <u>BEFORE JOHN</u>: 1
DAYS ON MARKET <u>BEFORE JOHN</u>: 311
WITH JOHN: SOLD – 6 DAYS – 98% Asking Price

CASE #4: 2418 E. COLONIAL DRIVE
NUMBER OF AGENTS <u>BEFORE JOHN</u>: 2
DAYS ON MARKET <u>BEFORE JOHN</u>: 387
WITH JOHN: SOLD – 5 DAYS – 105% Asking Price

CASE #1: 224 HOMESTEAD ROAD
NUMBER OF AGENTS <u>BEFORE JOHN</u>: 2
DAYS ON MARKET <u>BEFORE JOHN</u>: 90
WITH JOHN: SOLD – 37 DAYS – 95% Asking Price

No Seller Left Behind
How to Take the Stress Out of Distressed Sales

In 2006 we had decided to leave No Seller Left Behind by creating our **Distressed Sellers Division**.

When the economy turned, many sellers found themselves upside down on their mortgage. Whether it was a loss of job, divorce or death, we wanted a way to help those in need. No one should feel like a prisoner to their home.

If you find yourself in this position, here is what we recommend. Investigate your options. Speak with your lender *as soon as* you start experiencing financial difficulty. Don't let fear or embarrassment keep you from talking to the bank or mortgage company, as they must be put on notice of your situation. Remember that they want to avoid foreclosure as well.

Next, collect documentation outlining your current financial situation, and give it to the bank. You should provide income tax returns from the last two years, as well as recent bank statements. In addition to the numbers, you should also prepare a hardship letter. This letter will explain what's going on in your financial and personal life, and why you need their help.

It is also wise to speak with an attorney about your situation, as well as an experienced real estate professional. Please keep in mind, just because someone has a real estate license does not mean they can handle this type of situation. If you choose the wrong agent, it will undoubtedly cost you time, money, stress and potentially your home to foreclosure.

Alternatives to Foreclosure:

- Short Sales
- Forbearance Agreement
- Deed in Lieu of Foreclosure
- Certified Distressed Property Expert
- Help for Absentee Homeowners
- Loan Modification

Short Sales

Short sales, also known as pre-foreclosure sales, were once a fairly rare occurrence. Today however, short sales are on the rise as more people find themselves in over their heads with their mortgage.

When a homeowner sells their home for less than is owed on the mortgage, this is known as a short sale. The bank must approve of a short sale, and determine whether they will forgive the remaining balance or negotiate repayment with the seller.

Short sales are desirable because sellers are able to escape foreclosure, and in many cases, have a portion (or all) of their debt forgiven. For homeowners struggling to stay financially afloat, a short sale can offer great relief.

Short sales can be tricky due to the requirement of lender approval. Pre-foreclosure sales often take months to go through—if at all. The bank wants to get all their money back, so if they think they can recoup more money through foreclosure, they will deny the short sale. Unfortunately, with short sales, homeowners are at the mercy of their lenders, which can make the process stressful and time consuming. That said, homeowners that are in financial trouble should try for a short sale despite the chance that it might not be approved. A short sale will still leave a mark on one's credit score, but it won't be as detrimental as a foreclosure.

Loan Modification

If you want to remain in your house, but can't keep up with the payments, speak with your bank about the possibility of modifying your home loan. I must say, I have yet seen a successful loan modification. One option is to extend the length of the loan, so that the monthly payments become more manageable. There's also the possibility of shifting the mortgage from an adjustable rate to a fixed rate loan, in order to decreasing the amount of interest being charged from month to month. If you're already behind on your payments, the bank may attach the amount you're behind to the principal of the loan, to help you get current on your payments.

Include with your application detailed information about your income and assets, as well as a hardship letter.

Forbearance Agreement

If you're behind on your payments due to a temporary hardship, such as illness, you can apply for a forbearance agreement, which stops the bank from starting the foreclosure process. Forbearance gives you a few months to catch up on your mortgage by either extending your mortgage term, temporarily halting payments, reducing payments over the short term, or by temporarily increasing your payments until the outstanding amount is paid back. A hardship letter explaining why you're behind is required, as is a detailed financial statement.

Deed in Lieu of Foreclosure

A deed in lieu of foreclosure is when a homeowner hands over the deed to their home to the bank. Homeowners can apply for a deed in lieu of foreclosure if their loan has gone into default, there are no other liens against the property, and it appears that foreclosure is imminent. In exchange for handing over the deed, the bank will cancel the mortgage, and stop the foreclosure process. This does not guarantee, however, that the lender will forgive the balance of the loan. You'll need to negotiate with the bank to handle the outstanding balance.

The prospect of facing foreclosure can be overwhelming for homeowners already experiencing financial difficulties. It's imperative to have a support team that understands what you're going through, and can assist you with selling your home before the foreclosure process begins.

Short sales can be quite complicated, and not all real estate agents are familiar with them. We have over 50 years of combined experience and specialized training in short sales and foreclosure alternatives. I have experience not only in navigating the technical aspects of a short sale, but I also understand the emotional strain that homeowners in this situation can feel.

As your agent, I'm here to support and guide you as you try to sell your home.

Absentee Homeowners

In addition to helping distressed sellers, I also work with a number of absentee homeowners who need to sell their home at a distance. In many cases, these homeowners were unable to keep up with their mortgages, and were forced to rent out their properties while they relocated somewhere else. If it had been possible, they would've sold their homes rather than rent them out, however, they were unable to find the right buyer at the time. Now they're stuck dealing with tenants, and are attached to a home they can no longer afford.

In other cases, second homeowners have found themselves struggling to make ends meet, but are unable to sell their vacant home. The possibility of foreclosure looms, and the financial burden continues.

What Senior Citizens Should Know About Selling Their Home

When you are ready to retire, your home could be one of your most valuable assets. Therefore, selling your house at retirement age presents a different set of considerations than when you were younger. Whether you're downsizing, buying in a new community or moving in with family, it takes careful planning to get the most out of your equity.

Seek Specialized Real Estate Assistance

It is critical to find a real estate broker knowledgeable about the specialized needs of seniors. This is why we created a Senior Citizen Division at The JRS Realty Group. Through our experience and specialized training our agents are familiar with senior housing options, the Housing for Older Persons Act, possible schemes and scams and the implications of various financial transactions. As specialists, we can guide you in making appropriate sales decisions and refer you to other experts as needed.

Know Your Home's Current Value

Having lived in your home for many years, it is natural to be unsure of its current value. However, lack of knowledge about current prices could cause you to accept much less for your home than it's worth. You also might wait too long to accept a fair offer under the mistaken belief that a higher one may be around the corner. To find out the current price for your home, so that you don't lose out on a sale, review the comparative market analysis, or CMA, provided by a real estate professional. The CMA, compiled from data in our multiple listing service or MLS includes the most up-to-date information about homes in your neighborhood, similar to yours, that have sold

Investigate Incentives and Pitfalls

As a senior, you should be aware of the pitfalls and incentives associated with buying and selling a home at this point in your life. Seek advice from your financial adviser about the consequences of these transactions. Pensions, IRA accounts, Medicare, Medicaid, Social Security and estate planning could be impacted by a real estate sale. Additionally, should you plan to buy a new home in a retirement community, you could be eligible for perks such as reduced upfront fees and closing-cost assistance, depending on the community.

Pack Up Memories and Valuables

Selling your home presents an ideal time to sort through your belongings. "De-cluttering," a term used by real estate agents, means removing knick-knacks, excess furniture and family photos from your home before putting it on the market. De-cluttering makes a house look spacious and helps potential buyers picture their belongings in the house rather than yours. You may have accumulated many mementos through the years that you may wish to sell, giveaway to family members or donate before moving. While the house is on the market, keep items you wish to retain in storage. Valuables, medications and other personal items should be kept out of sight as well.

I know that sifting and sorting through a lifetime's worth of belongings and memories can be extremely difficult, so we have added services specific to senior needs. Seniors that work with us have access to:

• Presale home inspection services
• Staging services
• Professional organizing and de-cluttering services
• Assistance with the sale and donation of unwanted items
• Life transition and special counseling services.

Seniors who take advantage of the senior services division ultimately save money on moving and packing as well as eliminate stress. In the end, they get the highest possible sales price for their home in the shortest period of time.

PART FIVE

PUTTING IT ON PAPER

OFFERS, CONTINGENCIES ... CLOSING!

All About Offers, Counter Offers, and Contingencies

Congrats! You have an offer!

Once an offer is received, the next step is to decide whether to accept it, counter it or reject it.

I never suggest we reject an offer. If you are not satisfied with the offer, I highly suggest you counter. Regardless of how low or how outlandish the contingencies can be, the most important thing to remember is to not take anything personal. You must remain level-headed and let your decisions be guided by rationale, not emotion.

The offer will consist of a date, amount of earnest or good faith money, price, loan terms, a closing deadline, acceptance date, inspection contingencies and any other special requests. You, the seller, may like the price, terms and conditions and want to accept the offer. Or, you can ask for guidance from your broker on what he/she thinks. If you do not like the price, terms and condition than you and your broker will discuss how to respond via a counter offer. Keep in mind, once a counter offer is made; the initial offer no longer exists. I always urge my clients to come from a position of a win-win.

It has been tried and tested that to have a successful negotiation each party involved must feel like they won. This takes skill and expertise on behalf of your agent. Once you counter, they can accept, decline, or come back with a counter to your counter offer. Neither party is obligated to accept a counter offer.

Contingencies

Contingencies are conditions written into real estate offers and contracts so that you don't ultimately have to buy a house that is unsatisfactory.

Contingencies are very common in offers and almost always exist. The most common contingency is a property inspection contingency. The buyer will in most cases hire a professional inspector to examine the electric, plumbing, roof, windows, heating and cooling units for example. If they find anything that requires repair, the buyer has a few options. They may ask to be credited, or ask you to fix the problem before settlement and move-in date.

Financing-related contingencies are also very common. This involves the buyers being approved and qualified for a mortgage loan and appraisal.

Another common contingency is the buyer may need to sell their home first, thus submitting a sale and settlement contingency.

Some things to keep in mind regarding counter offers and contingencies, you as a buyer, must be careful not to demand too much. The seller may not want to move forward with your offer. The most important aspect of this phase of the home selling/buying process is to make this a win-win for all parties involved.

What You Need To Know About Closing

Closing or settlement is the final phase of the home selling/buying process. The professional you hired should have prepared you for this important step.

The closing process includes:

- **Selection of a Title Company**. The title company is chosen by the buyer.

- **Title Search and Insurance**. This is performed by the title company to assure there aren't any liens and/or judgments on the seller's property.

- **Loan Payoff Information**. If you have a mortgage, home equity loan, or other liens on your property, the title company or the seller's conveyance department will help get current balances and instructions to pay off the debts for the closing.

- **Preparation and Recording of Documents**. The title company will draw up a deed that the seller signs to legally transfer title to the buyers. When the closing is completed, the deed is recorded in the county courthouse where the home is located.

Estimate of Seller's Closing Costs

The typical closing costs incurred by the seller include:

- Buyer Broker Fee: 3 percent
- Listing Broker Fee: 3 percent
- Title Fee: $35

- Transfer Tax: 1% of sale price, however certain counties charge different amounts.
- Processing and Compliance Fee: $695 and may vary depending on brokerage
- Recording Fees: $40
- Express Mail Payoff Fee: $35
- Notary Fee: $35
- Resale Docs (for HOA): $100 to $250
- Use & Occupancy (U&O): $50 to $150
- Tax and Sewer Certificates: $150

Estimate of Buyer's Closing Costs

Some of the typical closing costs incurred by the buyer include:

- Appraisal Fee: $350+
- Credit Report: $50
- Loan Origination Fee: About 1 percent of loan cost
- Points: If you choose to purchase points to lower your rate.
- Title Insurance: $1,400 (based on $200,000 sale)
- Endorsements of Title Policy: $200 to $250
- Transfer Tax: 1% of sale price, however certain counties charge different amounts.
- Processing and Compliance Fee: $695 and may vary depending on brokerage
- Underwriting Fee: $300
- Flood Certification: $25
- Notary: $35
- Recording Fees: $200
- Tax Adjustments (Tax Escrow): twelve months of taxes.

The above fees are for illustration only. We suggest you have your real estate professional provide you with their estimate.

PART SIX

MOVING ON UP!

GEARING UP FOR THE BIG DAY

Even the most organized person can be unprepared for all that comes along with moving, so helping your clients out in any way will be greatly appreciated.

Moving Checklist

The best way to prepare clients for a move is by giving them this checklist, along with a calendar with their moving day marked on it. This will help keep them on track to make a smooth transition, as well as keep your information readily available to them if they have any questions or want to for refer your services to a friend.

✓ One to Two Months Prior to the Move:

- Decide if you are going to be using a moving company or if you are going to do it yourself.
- If you decide to use a moving company, make an appointment for the movers to come to your house to evaluate the work that will be needed and to give you an estimate.
- If you are going to be doing the move yourself, call a moving vehicle rental company to get their rates and reserve a truck for your big day.

✓ One Month Prior to the Move:

- Change your address with the post office, credit card companies, banks and magazine subscriptions.
- Call your current utility company and let them know what day to have your utilities disconnected (usually the day after your move). Call your new utility company to tell them what day to connect the utilities at your new home.
- Check with your insurance company to make sure the items you are moving will be covered.
- Create a list of friends, relatives and business associates who should be notified about your move.
- Transfer or get copies of medical and dental records for everyone in your family. Also, ask if they have any referrals for healthcare providers in the area you will be moving to.
- If you have children, get copies of school records, and if you have pets, get copies of the records from your veterinarian.
- Start going through your belongings and deciding what will be moved, sold or donated. Have a garage sale or sell your items online. For the items that will be donated, call your local charity and ask what the process is for donating the items.

- Purchase packing supplies and start filling an "Open First" box. This box will contain the items that you will need right away, such as toilet paper, soap, toothpaste, trash bags, cups and plates, scissors and snacks.
- Start a box for your valuables and important documents. Keep this box with you during your move.

✓ **Two to Three Weeks Prior to the Move:**

- Make any travel arrangements or special arrangements for any children or pets.
- If you are not using movers, start boxing items that you will not need before your move. Make sure to label the boxes for the room that they will go into at your new home, and if possible, make a list of what is in each box to create a master list.
- Begin using up your food in your pantry and refrigerator/freezer.

✓ **One Week Prior to the Move:**

- Confirm your reservation with the moving company or rental truck company.
- Transfer your prescriptions.
- Send out change of address notifications to the friends, relatives and business associates that you listed.

✓ **One Day Prior to the Move:**

- Make sure you have bottles of water and snacks for moving day, as everything will be packed.
- Pack your suitcase with your personal items and clothing you will need immediately.

✓ **Moving Day:**

- If you hired a moving company, supervise the movers. If you are moving yourself, communicate the plan for loading the rental truck to all who are helping you.
- Take a last look around to see that nothing is left behind.

THE JRS REALTY GROUP
REAL ESTATE ADVISORS

<u>Seller Utilities Checklist and Costs</u>

Date: _____

Seller: _____

Property Address:

_____

_____

Gas/Electric Company: _____
Cost: _____ (A,Q,M) - Natural Gas or Propane (circle one)

Oil Company: _____
Cost: _____ (A,Q,M)

Water Company:

_____

Cost: _____ (A,Q,M)

Sewer Authority: _____
Cost: _____ (A,Q,M)

Trash Company: _____
Cost: _____ (A,Q,M) - Private or Municipal (circle one)

HOA/Condo Association: _____ Cost: _____
(A,Q,M)

HOA/Condo Assoc. One Time Capital Contribution: _____

Comcast or Verizon? (circle one)

A – Annual   Q – Quarterly   M – Monthly

✓ **One Week After the Move:**

- Make sure your mail is being delivered properly.
- Change your automobile registration and driver's license.

Tips for Working with Professional Movers

Moving Doesn't Have to Be Stressful

Yes, moving can be complicated, but there is no reason to get stressed out. With a little research and planning you can avoid moving scams and eliminate much of the stress associated with a long-distance move. Here are some suggestions to avoid a stressful move:

1. **Talk to Friends**
   A good moving company is going to have happy customers eager to share an opinion. Look to social media or ask friends if they have had positive experiences with any moving companies.

2. **Find a Trusted Advisor**
   Talk to local real estate agents or home improvement contractors who work with movers every day. They can offer a professional perspective.

3. **Dust off the Yellow Pages**
   It is important to recognize that not all moving company websites represent legitimate moving companies. Your local phone book can help you find established moving companies with actual physical addresses and real brick and mortar offices.

4. **Check Business Credentials**
   Once you've made a list of prospective movers, contact each company and get their full legal name and 'doing business as' (DBA) names, the number of years in business, DOT and MC license numbers. With credentials in hand, you can reference FMCSA resources like protectyourmove.gov or SaferSys.org to see if a mover is federally licensed.

Obtaining Price Estimates

Reputable moving companies will comply with federal regulation requiring an in-home estimate. A representative will want to visit your home or facility in order to survey your goods and provide an estimate of cost. Be sure to schedule at least two visits so you have confidence in the estimates you receive.

Beware of estimates given over the phone or internet without a visual survey. The way you describe your belongings and the way a moving company views them could differ, leading to changes in pricing. A face-to-face meeting will clarify these points and help to ensure accurate pricing from the beginning.

During the estimate, take time to show the representative every item you wish to have moved. It is easy to overlook items in the basement, attic or in storage. The mover should be asking you probing questions so they can price the job accurately and adequately prepare for the move. You should feel free to ask any questions to assure your confidence in the company.

Inquire about "valuation" options. The valuation option you choose determines the mover's maximum liability for loss or damage caused by their handling and transportation. The liability of a mover for loss or damage is based upon the mover's tariffs, as well as federal laws and regulations, and has certain limitations and exclusions.

Don't Fall Victim to Moving Scams!

Did you know that approximately 3,000 Americans are affected by moving fraud every year?

Most often, rogue operations offer low initial estimates, then hold a victim's possessions hostage until they receive additional payments. You can avoid falling victim to scams by looking for the following red flags:

1. **Don't Offer a Deposit**
   Legitimate movers should never ask for a deposit before moving your items.

2. **Check the Physical Address**
   Check moving companies' websites and the phone book to ensure they have a physical address in your area. Having a residential address, no address, or just listing a P.O. Box could be an indicator the business is not legitimate.

3. **Verify an Active License**
    Look for a U.S. DOT number on the companies' website. All moving companies should have active operating authority and adequate insurance.

4. **Check Service Records**
    Check a company's reputation and qualifications with organizations like American Moving and Storage Association (AMSA) and the Better Business Bureau (BBB).

What To Do When Moving Scams Occur

Unfortunately, some consumers will still fall victim to rogue operators this year. Fortunately, there is a service called MoveRescue available to help. Those who feel they may have been scammed should contact MoveRescue at 800-832-1773. Consumers who call this number will talk to a representative who will assess the situation and direct the caller through the appropriate next steps. MoveRescue serves as a central source for consumers who need moving assistance or anti-fraud information.

Packing Tips

Use the right size boxes.
Put heavy items, like books, in small boxes; light items, like linens and pillows, in bigger ones. (Large boxes packed with heavy items are a common complaint of professional movers. They not only make the job harder but also have a better chance of breaking.)

Put heavier items on the bottoms of boxes, lighter items on top.
And if you're loading the truck yourself, pack heavier boxes first, toward the front of the truck, for balance.

Don't leave empty spaces in the boxes.
Fill in gaps with clothing, towels, or packing paper. Movers often won't move boxes that feel loosely packed or unbalanced.

Avoid mixing items from different rooms in the same box.
It will make your packing quicker and your unpacking a lot easier, too.

Label each box with the room it's destined for and a description of its contents.
This will help you and your movers know where every box belongs in your

new place. Numbering each box and keeping an inventory list in a small notebook is a good way to keep track of what you've packed—and to make sure you still have everything when you unpack.

Tape boxes well.

Use a couple of pieces of tape to close the bottom and top seams, then use one of the movers' techniques—making a couple of wraps all the way around the box's top and bottom edges, where stress is concentrated.

If you're moving expensive art, ask your mover about special crating.

Never wrap oil paintings in regular paper; it will stick. For pictures framed behind glass, make an X with masking tape across the glass to strengthen it and to hold it together if it shatters. Then wrap the pictures in paper or bubble wrap and put them in a frame box, with a piece of cardboard between each framed piece for protection.

Bundle breakables.

As you pack your dishes, put packing paper around each one, then wrap bundles of five or six together with more paper. Pack dishes on their sides, never flat. And use plenty of bunched-up paper as padding above and below. Cups and bowls can be placed inside one another, with paper in between, and wrapped three or four in a bundle. Pack them all in dish-barrel boxes.

Consider other items that will need special treatment.

Vansant says his movers treat TVs like any other piece of furniture, wrapping them in quilted furniture pads. He points out, however, that plasma TVs require special wooden crates for shipping if you don't have the original box and can be ruined if you lay them flat. If you're packing yourself, double-box your TV, setting the box containing the TV into another box that you've padded with packing paper.

REAL ESTATE DICTIONARY

Adjustments: Adjustments may be property taxes (either unpaid or paid in advance), sewer, condo fees, or mortgage interest already paid out for future service. These must be prorated and credited on closing to the buyer or seller as appropriate. This can involve an expenditure of several hundreds of dollars payable on the closing date when the sale is completed.

Agreement of purchase and sale (offer to purchase): A contract by which one party agrees to sell and another agrees to purchase. The contract may be first (no conditions attached) or conditional (certain conditions must be fulfilled).

Appraisal: The act of estimating value. An appraisal is performed for mortgage lending purposes and may not necessarily match the sale price of the property.

Assessed value: A valuation placed upon property by the county as a basis for municipal taxation. This may not be the same as market value.

Buy down: The seller effectively lowers the rate of interest of a mortgage by prepaying a portion of the interest on his own existing mortgage or on a mortgage arranged by the buyer.

Chattels: Personal property that is tangible and moveable—appliances, blinds, light fixtures, etc.

Closing date: The date specified in the Agreement of Sale when the buyer is to deliver the balance of money due and the seller is to deliver a duly executed deed and vacate the property (unless otherwise agreed).

Commission: Percentage of the home's sale price paid at closing to the listing agent and to cooperating agents.

Condition: A term in a contract that calls for a specific event or performance of some act before the agreement becomes firm and binding on all the parties.

Conditional offer: An Agreement of Sale may be subject to specific conditions. These conditions could be the arranging of a mortgage, a home inspection, or the selling of an existing home. There is always a time limit stipulated within which the specific conditions must be met.

Deed: The final document prepared by a title company or lawyer to be signed by the seller and buyer transferring ownership. This document is then registered against the property as evidence of ownership.

Deposit: Payment of money or other valuable consideration as pledge for fulfillment of contract.

Designated agent: Represents the interests of the party to the transaction for whom the licensee has been designated.

Dual agent: Acts as an agent for both the buyer and seller in the same transaction; takes no action that is adverse or detrimental to either party's interest in a transaction.

Easement: The right acquired for access to or over another person's land for a specific purpose, such as for a driveway or public utility.

Effective date: The date that the offer, from either the buyer or seller, is good until. It is typically "same day the offer is signed," or up to forty-eight hours after the signing (or counter-signing) date.

Encroachment: The unauthorized extension of boundaries of land (when a homeowner puts up a fence over the lot line and "takes over" some of the neighbor's property).

Encumbrances: Outstanding claim or lien recorded against property or any legal right to the use of the property by another person who is not the owner.

Fair market value: The highest price in terms of money that the property will bring to a willing seller if exposed for sale on the open market while allowing a reasonable time to find a willing buyer, buying with the knowledge of all the uses, and with neither party acting under necessity, compulsion, or peculiar and special circumstances.

Foreclosure: The right of a mortgagee to force the sale of the property should default occur.

Holdback: An amount of money withheld by the lender during the progress of construction of a house to ensure that construction is satisfactory at every stage. The amount of the holdback is generally equivalent to the estimated cost to complete construction.

Home inspection: The examination of the house by an expert selected by the buyer or seller.

Insurance: Before the transaction can be closed, the buyer must have property insurance arranged and in effect. Depending upon the area, this insurance must cover items such as fire, earthquake, flood, or hurricanes. Your title and mortgage companies, at the closing, will require a certificate from the insurance company.

Irrevocable: Incapable of being recalled or revoked; unchangeable, unalterable.

Mortgage discharge: The removal of all mortgages and other encumbrances by paying all outstanding liens against the property.

Option agreement: A document stipulating that, in exchange for a deposit, a specified individual is to be given first chance of buying a property in a specified period of time. If the option holder does not buy within the specified time, he loses his deposit.

Owner's net equity: The difference between the price for which a property could be sold and the total debts (mortgages or liens) registered against it.

Permanent fixtures: Permanent improvements to property that may not be removed upon the sale of the property (furnace, central air conditioning, pool, windows, etc.).

Prospect: A potential buyer or customer.

Real estate: Includes property, leasehold, and business, whether with or without the building, fixtures, stock-in-trade, goods, or chattels in connection with the operation of the business.

Real estate broker or salesperson: An intermediary between the buyer and seller who is licensed to carry out such activities.

Real property: The combination of tangible and intangible attributes of land and improvements. Value-wise, it is the sum of the value of the real estate, considered as land and structure and, for example, the tangible value arising by reason of a favorable lease. That is, the real estate plus the rights that go with it.

Salesperson (sales representative): An employee of an independent contractor or a broker authorized to trade in real estate (your agent).

Settlement statement: A statement of the financial breakdown of the transaction prepared by the title company for the seller setting out, in balance sheet form, the credits to the seller (i.e., purchase price, prepaid taxes, prepaid insurance, etc.), the credits to the buyer (i.e., deposits, arrears in taxes prior to the date of closing), and the balance due on closing.

Survey: The accurate mathematical measurement of land and buildings thereon, made with the aid of instruments.

Title: The means of evidence by which the owner of land has lawful ownership thereof.

ANNUAL HOME MAINTENANCE

A CHECKLIST FOR THE SEASONS

These are checklists you can use and incorporate into your routine home maintenance plan. They are broken up into seasons.

Annually:
Hire a home inspector to perform a home maintenance inspection as part of your routine home maintenance plan.

In the Spring:

- ✓ Check for damage to your roof
- ✓ Check all fascia and trim for deterioration
- ✓ Have a professional air conditioning contractor inspect and maintain your system as recommended by the manufacturer
- ✓ Check your water heater
- ✓ Replace all extension cords that have become brittle, worn or damaged
- ✓ Check your fire extinguishers
- ✓ Clean the kitchen exhaust hood and air filter
- ✓ Review your fire escape plan with your family
- ✓ Repair all cracked, broken or uneven driveways and walks to help provide a level walking surface
- ✓ Check the shutoff valve at each plumbing fixture to make sure they function
- ✓ Clean clothes dryer exhaust duct, damper, and space under the dryer
- ✓ Inspect and clean dust from the covers of your smoke and carbon monoxide alarms

In the Summer:

- ✓ Check kids playing equipment
- ✓ Check your wood deck or concrete patio for deterioration
- ✓ Check the nightlights at the top and bottom of all stairs
- ✓ Check exterior siding
- ✓ Check all window and door locks
- ✓ Check your home for water leaks
- ✓ Check the water hoses on the clothes washer, refrigerator icemaker and dishwasher for cracks and bubbles

In the Fall:

- ✓ Check your home for water leaks
- ✓ Have a heating professional check your heating system every year

- ✓ Protect your home from frozen pipes
- ✓ Run all gas-powered lawn equipment until the fuel is gone
- ✓ Test your emergency generator
- ✓ Have a certified chimney sweep inspect and clean the flues and check your fireplace damper
- ✓ Remove bird nests from chimney flues and outdoor electrical fixtures
- ✓ Inspect and clean dust from the covers of your smoke and carbon monoxide alarms
- ✓ Make sure the caulking around doors and windows is adequate to reduce heat/cooling loss
- ✓ Make sure that the caulking around your bathroom fixtures is adequate to prevent water from seeping into the sub-flooring

In the Winter:

- ✓ Clean the gutters and downspouts
- ✓ Confirm firewood at least 20 feet away from your home
- ✓ Remove screens from windows and install storm windows
- ✓ Familiarize responsible family members with the gas main valve and other appliance valves
- ✓ Clean the clothes dryer exhaust duct, damper and space under the dryer
- ✓ Make sure all electrical holiday decorations have tight connections
- ✓ Clean the kitchen exhaust hood and air filter
- ✓ Check the water hoses on the clothes washer, refrigerator icemaker and dishwasher for cracks and bubbles
- ✓ Check your water heater
- ✓ Test all AFCI and GFCI devices

SOME FINAL WORDS

At the outset of this book, I mentioned there are several reasons why someone decides to sell their home. And the most important reason?

YOUR reason.

This is a process. An absolute process.

It's confusing. It's complicated.

You don't need rhetoric. And you really don't need to hire someone you never hear from after they secure your listing. You need someone who has a proven track record and a plan. You need a professional who can sell your home. You want someone who will negotiate, price, market and communicate.

I invite you to contact me directly. I don't hide behind a phone number. I sincerely believe once we speak and meet, you will see for yourself what differentiates me from other agents. It's my hope I can earn your trust.

I want to say thank you for taking the time to read this book. I hope you have found answers to some lingering questions. And if by chance I missed one, I truly hope you will reach out.

I look forward to hearing from you. Please call me at 610-709-5147 or pass along an email to me at John@JRSRealtyGroup.com.

- John

TRUSTED ADVISORS

JAMES CARNEY, JR.
DEL-VAL HOME INSPECTORS, INC.

James Carney, Jr. is a well-respected and sought-after home inspector in southeastern Pennsylvania.

After spending more than 20 years in custom home building and commercial construction, Jim forged a natural transition into home inspection. He was introduced to his new career path through a highly experienced inspector who mentored him through hundreds of home inspections before deciding to start Del-Val Home Inspectors Inc., in 2012. During this time, he took numerous classes, specializing in radon and termite testing, becoming certified through the American Society of Home Inspectors, where he is currently a board member.

With continued growth over the past five years, Del Val Home Inspectors, also performs water sampling and mold testing for buyers, providing a one-stop source for most home inspection needs. The company also works with sellers to perform pre-listing inspections prior to sale to avoid any surprises at closing time.

Jim and his team keep the interest of the client in mind, evaluating each property as if it was a home they are buying, so that everyone has the ability to make an informed decision with their investment. Del Val Home Inspectors' honesty, integrity and hard work, many real estate agents will only recommend Jim and his team's services for their clients.

If you would like to contact Jim directly, call 215-850-3819, email him at jim@delvalhi.com or visit their website at delvalhi.com.

BILL ROOKSTOOL
APPROVED MORTGAGE GROUP

Bill Rookstool is a mortgage banker running the Approved Mortgage Group team and the retail division of Approved Mortgage Group, a division of Florida Capital Bank N.A.

He has been in the mortgage industry for 13 years with offices in Doylestown, Philadelphia, Coatesville and Reading. His team consists of top originators that specialize in working with first-time home buyers and mortgage advice. As an active investor and developer, he supports his community by offering seminars for home buyers and investors. He also provides training and workshops for the local Realtors.

The AMG team approach allows us to provide the highest level of customer service and an on-time closing guarantee. AMG also provides a $2,500 guarantee on pre-approvals to the seller of a home. This gives the seller confidence in the closing of the mortgage and buyers a big competitive edge in a multiple offer situation. Referrals from satisfied customers are a very important part of AMG's business. AMG's goal is to earn a client's confidence and become their trusted mortgage advisor for years to come.

AMG Team specialties include: Purchase and Refinance Mortgages, FHA Mortgages, VA Mortgages, USDA Mortgages, PHFA Mortgages, Construction Lending, 203K Mortgages, Grant Programs, PHFA Loans, Jumbo Mortgages, Mortgage advice to home buyers.

To contact Rookstool directly, he can be reached by phone at 215-622-9779 or by email at bill@approvedmortgagegroup.com.

DANIEL KANE
KANE INSURANCE GROUP, LLC

Daniel Kane is the Principal and Owner of Kane Insurance Group, LLC, located in King of Prussia, Pennsylvania.

Kane Insurance Group is an independent insurance agency that assists clients and businesses in managing the risks of everyday life. The agency represents 15 different companies and works with all lines of insurance – auto, home, life, commercial, and health. Kane Insurance Group is licensed in Pennsylvania, New Jersey, Delaware, Maryland, Ohio, and Florida, allowing further flexibility for clients looking to have one agency service all their needs.

Outside of work, Kane is actively engaged in the local community. He spearheads the planning for the local University of Richmond Alumni chapter, networks through the Bryn Mawr Running Club, and volunteers for his homeowners association board. In addition, he also started his own annual fundraiser to benefit the American Cancer Society after the loss of a close friend. To date - it's now raised more than $43,000.

He is always happy to assist and can be reached at 610-337-8100 or via email at dan@kaneig.com. More information about his agency can be viewed at www.kaneig.com.

MURRAY D. LEVIN, ESQ.
GRATEFUL ABSTRACT, LLC

Murray D. Levin, Esq., is the founder of Grateful Abstract, LLC.

After four years of teaching, Levin became an attorney in 1981 and began his career in banking and title insurance in 1984.

With more than three decades in the industry, he has been qualified as a title insurance expert witness in both, state and federal courts and has also spoken at numerous seminars approved by the Pennsylvania Land Title Association.

In addition, Levin has held elected office as a public school board president and vice president, as well as having served on nine boards of director in non-profit and for-profit ventures.

Having been responsible for more than 10,000 closings, Levin is most grateful for those mortgage lenders, bankers, Realtors, attorneys, consumers and friends that continue to refer business. His goal at every settlement is to hear these three words – "That was painless."

He holds a Master's Degree in Education from Arcadia University and a Juris Doctorate degree from the Rutgers School of Law.

To speak with Levin or to schedule an appointment, he can be reached at 215-887-7000 or via email at MDLESQ@gmail.com.

MIKE MITCHELL
DYNAMIC LANDSCAPING & IRRIGATION

Founded in 1985, Mike Mitchell founded Dynamic Landscaping and now with more than three decades of experience, Dynamic has grown into a highly-respected company which consistently ranks at the top of customer satifaction surveys.

With proficiency in hardscapes, softscapes, irrigation, lighting, outdoor kitchens and design, Mitchell and his team of landscape professional are equipped to handle any project. Dynamic is committed to producing, maintaining high-quality and competitively-priced solutions for private clients, construction contractors, property developers and commercial property owners.

Actively committed to their community Mitchell and Dynamic Landscaping support organizations and charities such as the Epilepsy Foundation of Eastern Pennsylvania, Omega Horse Rescue, Cure Tay-Sachs Foundation, the Philadelphia Animal Welfare Society, Women's Humane Society and Children's Hospital of Philadelphia.

Contact Dynamic by calling 215-757-4424. Find them on the internet at www.DynamicLandscape.com. And to contact Mitchell directly, email him at mmitchell@dynamiclandscape.com.

ABOUT THE AUTHOR

JOHN SALKOWSKI

JOHN SALKOWSKI
BROKER / OWNER – THE JRS REALTY GROUP

John Salkowski is a highly successful real estate broker based in King of Prussia, Pennsylvania. For more than a decade, John has headed The JRS Realty Group Real Estate Advisors as its founder, president and broker.

In addition to having distinguished himself among the top 1% of Realtors in the nation and Philadelphia Magazine for client satisfaction and customer service, John is a best-selling author of the book – *Leadership in the Line of Duty.*

John's road to real estate followed a somewhat indirect path. After 15 years as a police officer, John wanted to find a profession where he could have more control over his day-to-day activities.

As he tells it:

"The reason I made the switch to real estate was due to my entrepreneurial spirit and strong desire to build my schedule. I have been on my own and working since I was 13 – cutting lawns, snow shoveling – when my friends were out sledding and having snowball fights. Being an entrepreneur is in my DNA. I have always loved real estate. Ever since I can remember it was a dream of mine to have my own home. Real estate was a natural fit to go after my dream."

Using innovative marketing and state-of-the-art technology, John creates lead-generating websites for sellers who are looking to put their homes on the market. Working on the guarantee – *Your Home Sold in 45 Days or We'll Sell It for Free* – John and his team uses every available resource to create a database of more than 1,000 buyers actively searching for homes in the Great Philadelphia area.

Staying up-to-date on the constantly changing market, John regularly attends conferences and seminars nationwide to find unique buyer and seller programs.

His success and growth has not gone unnoticed, as he is regularly invited to speak and share his expertise to other real estate professionals and leadership experts.

Career Information:

Education
University of Alabama (Criminal Justice, 1992)
Montgomery County Community College (Associate's Degree, Criminal Justice – 1990)

Professional Memberships
Suburban West Realtors Association
National Association of REALTORS

Awards / Honors
Top 1% out of 40,000 Realtors for client satisfaction and customer services –
Philadelphia Magazine (2010-2016)
Top 250 Real Estate Professionals in America – Real Trends (2016)
Best-Selling Author – National Academy of Best-Selling Authors (2012)

Made in USA - North Chelmsford, MA
1065554_9781975994051
03.31.2020 1042